ISBN 978-0-359-74533-3

I0487955

Copyright © 1998-2019 On The Edge Software Consulting

Preface

 This book is based on an action research project I completed as part of my master's degree in Adult Education in 2010. In addition to my research I have 35 years of industry experience in software engineering and Information Technology that includes more than 10 years in technical management, 10 years in enterprise architecture, and 15 years building complex applications that ranged from embedded system applications, Windows ® desktop applications, and Enterprise web applications. I have held positions as a Test Engineer, Software Engineer, Solutions Architect, Enterprise Architect, Software Engineering Manager, Application Development Manager, and Director of Software. I am also the co-author of five patents. I left the industry in 2016 and am now a Professor employed as a full-time faculty member for the College of Science, Engineering, and Technology at Grand Canyon University.

The purpose of my original research in 2010 was to further understand the gaps in the current Computer Science and Information Technology programs in our colleges and universities. This research took place from the perspective of corporate America and could be used to provide valuable feedback to the college and university Computer Science and Information Technology programs. This book is written in the style of an action research paper. Chapters 1 through 3 are written in past tense and present a research proposal to the reader. Chapters 4 and 5 are written in present tense using research results to make recommendations to improve our Computer Science and Information Technology programs. My research was completed to help me further understand the reasons for the issues and struggles I faced as a hiring manager in the field of Information Technology and Software Development finding qualified entry level software developers for my software development and software engineering departments.

When I conducted my research in 2010, I asked myself the following questions. What could academia learn by studying our current software development teams already working professionally in corporate software engineering and Information Technology companies? What could academia learn from our recent college and university Computer Science graduates? Could academia use this information to identify gaps and provide constructive feedback to our colleges and universities to improve the quality of our education programs? My action research project provided research data to answer these questions. The research I completed helped debug our Computer Science and Information technology programs.

Chapters 6 and 7 were added as part of the 2nd edition of this book and is being written six years after the 1st edition was published. The 2nd edition reflects back on my original research in 2010 and documents how one major U.S. University has amazingly solved my research problem. It should be noted that when I originally performed my research, I had no affiliation with that U.S. University.

Table of Contents

My Action Research Project From 2012

Chapter 1: Research Overview

Introduction

This book is based on an action research project. The purpose of this research was to further understand the gaps in the recent Computer Science and Information Technology programs. This research takes place from the perspective of corporate America and can be used to provide valuable feedback to the college and university Computer Science and Information Technology (IT) programs. This book is written in the style of an action research project. Chapter I through IV are written in past tense and written in the style of a research proposal. Chapter V is written in present tense using the research results to make recommendations to improve our Computer Science and Information Technology programs.

When the research was conducted the following questions were asked. What could academia learn by studying our current software development teams already working professionally in corporate software engineering and Information Technology companies? What could academia learn from our recent college and university Computer Science graduates? Could academia use this information to identify gaps and provide constructive feedback to our colleges and universities to improve the quality of our education programs? The action research project provided research data to answer these questions. The research completed helped debug our Computer Science and Information technology programs.

Research Problem Statement

All research begins by defining a problem statement. This research study is no different. The following defines the research problem statement. The problem was that many college and university Computer Science graduates and Information Technology (IT) graduates are not properly prepared academically to maintain, design, and develop Enterprise class web applications.

Description of Research Community

Research was completed to identify potential gaps in the current Computer Science and Information Technology programs and use the perspective of a software development team working in corporate

America in a technology company who maintain, design, and build web-based applications to run their business.

The software development team members selected for this research project consisted of 13 software developers working professionally in a well-established 10-year-old $100M technology company located in the United States. The technology company has a total of 200 employees in the company's corporate headquarters and has an additional 100 employees who work remotely throughout the United States. All members of the software development team reside in the United States corporate office.

The 13 software developers were responsible for maintaining, designing, and building Microsoft .NET ® web applications. The software developers have an opportunity to grow into four different career paths spanning four different positions and titles within the department. The career levels range from software developer 1, software developer 2, software developer 3, and software architect. Each of the career levels has a varying degree of software design and development responsibilities. The software developer level 1 position is for developers from entry-level to 3 years of industry experience. The software developer level 2 position requires four to seven years of industry experience. The software developer level 3 position requires eight to 10 years of industry experience. The architect level requires greater than 10 years of industry experience. The profile of the software development team members consisted of three females and 10 males and the professional experience of the team ranged from three to 25 years. The team members with three to five years of industry experience made up 30% of the software development team. The team members with five to 10 years of industry experience made up 60% of the software development team. The team members with more than 10 years of industry experience made up 10% of the software development team.

The skills necessary by the development team to maintain, design, and build Microsoft .NET web applications require experience in the following technologies: C#, .NET3.5, SQL, HTML, JavaScript, and CSS.

Description of Research Work Setting

The software development team worked in a well-established 10-year-old $100M technology company in the United States. The entire team was made up of full-time salaried employees of the company. The software development team works locally in the United States corporate office but is allowed to work remotely from home two days a month. The technology company does not consider offshore development as an available development model because of licensing restrictions for some of the 3rd party software required to support the business applications.

The software development team works with the standard Microsoft .NET development tools to maintain, design, and build Microsoft .NET web applications. The Subversion open source framework and Microsoft Team Foundation Server are used as version control systems. Other tools leveraged by the software development team included SQL Navigator and TOAD, which are tools for working with a database. The software development team had access to the Microsoft Development Network (also referred to as MSDN), which is used to access technical resources and technical training classes.

The software development team works day-to-day under the direction of a development lead. The development lead reports to the Director of Software. The software development team works closely with the Project Management Office, Quality Assurance team, and the Information Technology team. The Director of Software is responsible for establishing training plans for the full-time employees of the software development team. The Director of Software has a minimal $10,000 annual budget for training the software development team. The Director of Software had established formal Personal Development Plans (PDP) for each of the members of the software development team. The Personal Development Plans are established annually and is used to establish a formal training plan and career plan for each member of the software development team.

Researchers Role

The author's role in the software development team was that of a Director of Software. The responsibility of the Director of Software included acting as a hiring manager for the software development department. Additional responsibilities of the Director of Software included establishing job requirements, staffing the software development team, setting technical and strategic direction for the team, establishing software development processes within the software development department, and establishing training plans for members of the team.

The author has more than 10 years' experience building and staffing software development teams. Staffing the software development teams included hiring college graduates and developers who have one to 10 years of experience maintaining, designing, and building software. The writer worked with staffing companies, job boards, and consulting companies to assist in searching for candidates to fill open job requisitions. Once potential job candidates are found the writer is responsible for reviewing the candidates job resume, setting up the interview process, interviewing the candidates, and ultimately selecting the candidates to fill the open job requisitions.

The author has 30 years of industry experience in software engineering and Information Technology. The 30 years of industry experience included more than 10 years in technical management, five years in enterprise architecture, and 15 years building complex applications that ranged from embedded systems, Windows desktop applications, and Enterprise web applications. The writer has held positions as a Test Engineer, Software Engineer, Solutions Architect, Enterprise Architect, Software Engineering Manager, Application Development Manager, and Director of Software. The writer is also the co-author of five patents. The writer maintains an online presence through a detailed website as well as leveraging professional social Internet sites such as LinkedIn ®.

Chapter 2: Study of the Problem

Problem Description

The problem was that many college and university Computer Science graduates and Information Technology (IT) graduates are not properly prepared academically to maintain, design, and develop Enterprise class web applications. Computer Science graduates and Information Technology graduates must be properly trained to maintain and build web applications.

Web applications have become predominantly used to implement almost all current desktop, business, mobile, and personal applications. The technologies used to build web applications are even used as the foundation to build applications for consumer devices, such as advanced TV set top boxes and digital TV's. The Enterprise Java platform and the Microsoft .NET platform are the major platforms of choice for many companies who need to build these web applications. Research was required to determine how to improve the curriculum, how to improve the hands-on programming labs, and how to better prepare Computer Science and Information Technology graduates for entry into the current workforce for companies looking to hire software developers to design and develop web applications. Additionally, this research was important because if Computer Science graduates are not qualified to design and develop Enterprise class web applications these programming positions will continue to be filled by using lower cost offshore outsource resources in countries, such as India and China.

One of the first primary responsibilities of most Computer Science and Information Technology graduates entering the professional workforce is to maintain software. Research was required to determine if the proper foundational skills are taught to maintain software in a professional environment.

Problem Documentation

Current research from 2005-2010 was used to identify current gaps in the Computer Science and Information Technology programs, which illustrated the urgency and importance of resolving these gaps.

One of the contributing factors causing the gaps in the Computer Science program is the declining enrollment rate in the program. Declining enrollment rates have reduced the capital investments, research, and grant funds the colleges and universities receive so they can continue to make advancements in the Computer Science program. One of the contributing factors in the declining enrollments is the impact of outsourcing the United States software development positions to countries such as India and China. Hoganson in 2004 researched the impacts of the movement of technical jobs, made recommendations, and suggested a strategy to improve the Computer Science program to counteract the impact of the offshore movement. Hoganson noted that Computer Science enrollments are off nationwide, due in part to the tech downturn, and due in part to the well-publicized movement of tech jobs overseas in a global economy with instantaneous communications. Computer Science program coordinators and curriculum committees are in a quandary: the organization and content of a science education should not be dependent upon the whims of the marketplace (Hoganson, 2004). These observations suggest that IT knowledge and skills are critical to a business enterprise, and hence more difficult to successfully outsource may form the basis for positioning computer science degree programs (Hoganson, 2004). Computer Science degree programs that capitalize on these observations to prepare their graduates with knowledge in areas that tend to be critical and strategic, may mitigate some of the effect of the outsourcing movement on their graduate's job prospects and on program enrollment (Hoganson, 2004).

The following research by Bagaya in 2007 further validated the urgency and need to improve the Computer Science and Information Technology curriculum.

- New Computer Science majors have declined 32% since 2000 (Bagaya, 2007).
- Computer Science programs are now viewed as a path to unemployment versus a path to wealth (Bagaya, 2007).
- The United States now has a shortage of IT and Computer Science skills (Bagaya, 2007).
- 62% of IT workers lost jobs because of business downturn, 80% of IT workers will not stay in the profession, an increase demand of 38% for IT workers, and 41% of IT workers would not recommend this profession (Bagaya, 2007).
- The circumstances and forces behind offshore outsourcing present a challenge to the United States historical lead in high-tech innovation (Bagaya, 2007).
- University administrators need to design undergraduate courses to attract new students and retain enrolled students (Bagaya, 2007).

IT managers may think that their new hires are ill-prepared for the real-world, but many higher education professionals refuse to shoulder the blame. At its heart, the issue revolves around two questions: the expectation of a college grad's knowledge, and the old art-versus-science debate about programming that you probably had in your own dorm room when you were in school (Schindler, 2005). Companies therefore must invest in extensive additional training beyond what graduates obtain as part of their college education programs. Most four-year programs still are trying to turn out Computer Science graduates who are prepared to move into any part of the field, or to go on to a research-oriented graduate program (Ward, 2010). Perhaps, said Ward that is not realistic. The Computer Science field is starting to fission into several separate specializations, much as engineering has. "We're seeing more schools offering 'tracks' of upper-division electives that allow students to gain some additional depth in one part of the field at the expense of others, and we're seeing more students turn to non-thesis masters degrees for additional specialization. We are also starting to see more specific four-year programs, such as software engineering degrees." There is also more emphasis on real-world skills in the generalist education (Schindler, 2005).

Software development companies or the graduates themselves must make a large initial investment in college graduates to compensate for the skills the graduates did not obtain in their Computer Science and Information Technology program. Enysnch Corporation, a premier Information Technology consulting company in the United States, recently has started a new training program within their company. The company hires new Computer Science and Information Technology program graduates and trains them internally with their own curriculum. This training is necessary because the graduates are not prepared to maintain, design, or build web applications. It is estimated that three to six man months of focused technical training is required by Ensynch to prepare the graduates to work in the industry. Ensynch makes an additional $25,000 investment in each graduate beyond what the graduate has already spent on a college or university degree. Other forms of training are available to Computer Science and Information Technology program graduates who wish to augment the skills they received in their college programs. For example, Oracle Corporation offers training and certification classes in the Enterprise Java platform. These certification classes generally cost thousands of dollars. Many of the foundational technical training classes offered by Ensynch or Oracle could be offered as part of a refreshed Computer Science and Information Technology curriculum.

Research was completed to identify the gaps in the Computer Science and Information Technology programs. A number of forms of documentation were used to identify the skills required when hiring new software developers who would be responsible for maintaining, designing, and building web applications. This inventory of skills obtained from the documentation sources were compared and contrasted to the current technologies, standards, and platform trends that have been used in the industry over the past five years to build Enterprise web applications. Other forms of documentation researched included the evaluation of resumes, job boards, research industry trade journals, blogs, and Internet sites used to monitor industry trends. By researching the current college and university programs the writer could assemble an inventory of the technologies, standards, and platforms taught in these programs. This inventory was compared and contrasted to the current technologies, standards, and platform trends used in the industry between 2005-2010 to build Enterprise web applications.

Additional research data was obtained by researching current development teams in the software development industry. What could academia learn by studying our current software development teams already working professionally in corporate software engineering and information technology companies? What could academia learn from our recent college and university Computer Science and Information Technology graduates? Could academia use this information to identify gaps and provide constructive feedback to our colleges and universities to improve the quality of our education programs? This action research project provided research data to answer these questions.

Literature Review

The importance, validation, and urgency of the problem statement were discovered in many literature resources. The following literature review summarizes the important research discoveries relevant to the problem statement. This research was conducted from 2005-2010.

Research shows that one of the major issues in the United States is the declining enrollment for new students in Computer Science and Information Technology programs. To make matters worse the supply for these skills in the workforce is on a rapid increase. The United States has a supply and demand problem for Computer Science and Information Technology resources. "Headlines about soaring oil prices and the iPhone's introduction signal that even more jobs will be created in such areas as alternative energy, online networking, and mobile technology, say recruiters. In response to rising gasoline prices, companies offering alternative-energy solutions are sprouting up, creating a need for workers with backgrounds in fields ranging from Marketing to Computer Science. Last year, search assignments for these types of companies accounted for 15% of some firm's business and it is expected to climb to 25% in 2008" (Needleman, 2007, p. 1). Unfortunately, the United States now has a shortage of Computer Science and IT skills and new Computer Science majors have declined 32% since 2000 (Bagaya, 2007). University administrators will need to design undergraduate courses to attract new students and retain enrolled students (Bagaya, 2007). "Undergraduate programs in IS (now referred to as IT) and Computer Science are struggling to keep pace with warp-speed technological and business changes. Many schools are lagging and widening the distance between buyers and suppliers of new IT talent. IT managers and recruiters say the disconnect has driven up training budgets, forced many companies to stop hiring new graduates, fueled outsourcing, and cost untold amounts in dollars and lost productivity as a result of mistakes by poorly trained IT workers" (Maglitta, 1996, p. 1).

One of the important factors that should be considered in Computer Science and Information Technology programs is to make sure the curriculum is aligned with the web programming platforms and programming languages currently used in the industry. It is important that Computer Science and Information Technology programs offer classes in Microsoft .NET and Java platforms as well as offer programming classes in Java and C#. Ivan Kedrin from NY CTO, who is an online web technologist, reports that more than 75% of job trends in 2011 demand the Enterprise Java platform or the Microsoft .NET platform. The

Microsoft .NET and Java platforms, as shown in the figure 1 below, are the most sought-after general software development technology stacks. Microsoft .NET currently represents about 3.5% of all job openings, while Java is around 3% of all job openings. These numbers are inflated by non-web application development jobs. The respective percentages that represent web application development done using both platforms should be significantly lower. Kedrin would not be surprised if less than 40% of total Java and Microsoft .NET development were web application development related, while the rest would fall into the client/server/other categories (Kedrin, 2011). Research from LangPop.org, as shown in figure 2 below, reports that Java and C# are among the top programming languages used in the industry. Initial research in 2010 from three of the top Computer Science programs in the United States, as reported by the GRE College Guide, shows that only a minimal number of classes ranging from program and development, Java, and C++ are offered as part of the program. Using information published from Gartner, a renowned technology research company, showed the following technology trends from 2006-2011. The information from Gartner provided further insight into the technologies that should be considered in current Computer Science and Information Technology programs.

a. 2006: Web 2.0 that includes AJAX and mash-ups, real-world web that includes location aware technologies, and application architecture that includes model-driven architecture.
b. 2007: Real-world web, virtual worlds and social networks, user interface enhancements, and mobile robots.
c. 2008: Virtualization, Cloud computing, servers-beyond blades, web-oriented architectures, Enterprise mash-ups, specialized systems, social software, social networking, unified communications, business intelligence, Green IT.
d. 2009: Virtualization, business intelligence, cloud-computing, Green IT, unified communications, social software, social networking, web-oriented architecture, Enterprise mash-ups, specialized systems, servers – beyond blades.
e. 2010: Cloud computing, advanced analytics, client computing, Green IT, reshaping the Data Center, social computing, security – activity monitoring, flash memory, virtualization for availability, mobile applications.
f. 2011: Cloud computing, mobile applications and media tablets, social communications and collaboration, video, next generation analytics, social analytics, context-aware computing, storage class memory, ubiquitous computing, fabric-based infrastructure, and fabric-based computers.

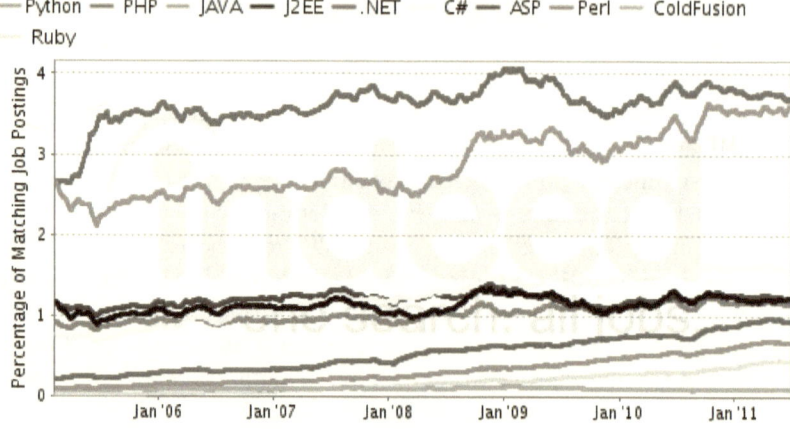

Figure 1. Job Trends in 2011

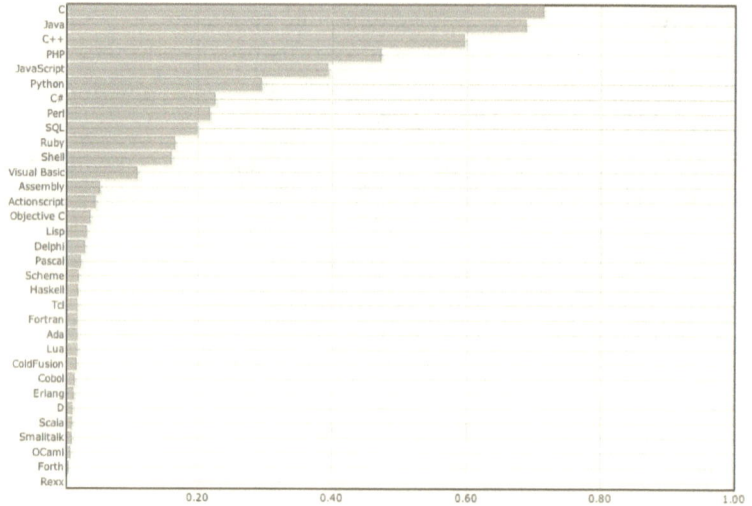

Figure 2. Programming Language Popularity

Research conducted in 2010 across eight Fortune 500 businesses, nine small-to-medium businesses, and two nonprofit organizations, using the results of 20 interviews that consisted of seven open-ended questions, across IT professionals, such as 6 Sigma Black Belts, Senior Project Analysts, Quality Assurance Analysts, Computer Scientists made the following recommendations.

a.   Modify Computer Science curriculum to provide more emphasis on written and verbal communication skills, gathering, and eliciting customer requirements effectively (Simmons, 2010).

b.   Provide the ability to be flexible and the ability to deal with varying personalities were highly emphasized (Simmons, 2010).

c.   Introduce negotiation skills, time management, and cultural differences; outsource management, and information assurance trainings as some of the most notable skills in addition to a strong technical background (Simmons, 2010).

The following summarizes the research by Bagaya in 2007 and further validated the urgency and need to improve the Computer Science and Information Technology curriculum. Bagaya discovered that the United States now has a shortage of IT and Computer Science skills and that one of the contributing factors in the decline of these skills in the United States is because of the outsourcing of these jobs. Bagaya suggested that administrators of universities need to design undergraduate courses to attract new students and retain enrolled students.

- New Computer Science majors have declined 32% since 2000 (Bagaya, 2007).
- Computer Science programs are now viewed as a path to unemployment versus a path to wealth (Bagaya, 2007).
- The United States now has a shortage of IT and Computer Science skills (Bagaya, 2007).
- 62% of IT workers lost jobs because of business downturn, 80% of IT workers will not stay in the profession, an increase demand of 38% for IT workers, and 41% of IT workers would not recommend this profession (Bagaya, 2007).
- The circumstances and forces behind offshore outsourcing present a challenge to the United States historical lead in high-tech innovation (Bagaya, 2007).
- University administrators need to design undergraduate courses to attract new students and retain enrolled students (Bagaya, 2007).

Industry leaders and editors of software development trade journals have made a number of observations, expressed concerns, and made recommendations to improve Computer Science and Information Technology programs. One of the popular software industry journals is Software Development Times. This monthly journal tracks the trends, technologies, and corporations in the software development industry. Recently the Software Development Times editors asked: What are Computer Science students taught? New hire graduates are asked to write software and one of their first responsibilities includes code maintenance.

Maintaining existing software is the quickest way to get up to speed, not only on the codebase itself but also on corporate coding practices. We propose a new course for all Computer Science majors. This course would be of code maintenance (SD Editorial Board, 2010). If one of the first responsibilities of new hire graduates of Computer Science and Information Technology programs is maintaining software the skills required to maintain software must be properly taught in our colleges and universities.

Keith Ward from the MSDN Magazine, a popular technology magazine on Microsoft technology, observed the following in 2010. Ward provided a quote from a hiring manager for a technology company who claimed "I have never interviewed a candidate right out of college who I would hire. No recent graduate that I have interviewed has had sufficient understanding of real-world problems to be useful to me, at least for the salary that the interviewees were expecting" (Ward, 2010, p. 1). Ward went on to suggest that the industry use the power of the MSDN network to help determine if we are facing a crisis when it comes to teaching college students proper software development skills (Ward, 2010). It is evident from observations like the one from the hiring manager that changes must be considered in the curriculum in the Computer Science and Information Technology programs in the United States.

An article by Esther Schindler from the Software Development Times, a popular technology magazine, observed the following in 2005. "I seemed to be engaged in a constant battle with most of them to obtain properly documented and readable code," she said. Few would follow even the most basic guidelines. Many did not have the habit of proper code development in the first place" (Dzikovska, 2005). IT managers may think that their new hires are ill-prepared for the real world, but many higher education professionals refuse to shoulder the blame. At its heart, the issue revolves around two questions: the expectation of a college grad's knowledge (and thus your company's need to provide additional training), and the old art-versus-science debate about programming that you probably had in your own dorm room when you were in school (Schindler, 2005). Most four-year programs still are trying to turn out Computer Science graduates who are prepared to move into any part of the field, or to go on to a research-oriented graduate program (Ward, 2010). Perhaps, said Ward that is not realistic. The Computer Science field is starting to fission into several separate specializations, much as engineering has. "We're seeing more schools offering 'tracks' of upper-division electives that allow students to gain some additional depth in one part of the field at the expense of others, and we're seeing more students turn to non-thesis master's degrees for additional specialization. We are also starting to see more specific four-year programs, such as software engineering degrees." There is also more emphasis on real-world skills in the generalist education (Schindler, 2005). Schindler and Ward both believe that Computer Science graduates are not properly prepared for entry into the workforce and suggest some of the blame be placed on higher education professionals.

An article by Bob Lewis from the InfoWorld Magazine, a popular technology magazine on computer technology, observed the following in 2010. This seems to be a trend: In an effort to widen and deepen my own skill set, I have had occasion to examine computer science course material available online from a number of top-tier colleges and some from the lower rungs. In most instances, what I remember from my nearly 40-year-old computer science education still places me far ahead of what they are now teaching; I had to search elsewhere (mostly in open source offerings or even now-old, but graduate-level textbooks) for suitable material (Lewis, 2010). We have had trouble finding qualified United States job applicants who want to do the work we need done. I wonder if there is a connection (Lewis, 2010). Lewis implied that Computer Science skills being taught in top-tier colleges are not on par with what the industry requires. Lewis went on to say that he could not find qualified job applications and questioned if there was a direct relationship between the skills being taught in the colleges and the challenges, he faced hired college graduates.

The literature review illustrates that industry professionals, trade journals, technical magazine editors, and researchers clearly validated and articulated the need to close the gaps in the Computer Science and Information Technology programs. It is evident after the literature review that the problem statement has supporting research and a major issue exists in the curriculum in the Computer Science and Information Technology programs. Research was completed to identify the gaps in the Computer Science and Information Technology programs.

Causative Analysis

A number of causes exist for the curriculum misalignment with the Computer Science and Information Technology programs and the needs of the software development industry.

One of the first issues discovered from the current research is the declining enrollment rate of the Computer Science and Information Technology programs in the United States. Enrollment rates are declining in part because the programs are outdated, and administrators of universityies need to design undergraduate courses to attract new students and retain enrolled students. Another contributing factor to the declining enrollment rates is the influence outsourcing United States programming positions to countries such as India and China. The United States must find creative approaches to improve the Computer Science and Information Technology programs, improve enrollment rates, and reduce the dependency on outsourced programming positions. Currently the Computer Science and Information Technology programs are not an attractive option for new students.

Web applications have become predominantly used to implement almost all current desktop, business, mobile, and personal applications. The technologies used to build web applications are even used as the foundation to build applications for consumer devices, such as advanced TV set top boxes and digital TV's. The Enterprise Java platform and the Microsoft .NET platform are the major platforms of choice for many companies who need to build these web applications. More than 75% of job trends in 2011 demand the Enterprise Java platform or the Microsoft .NET platform. The Microsoft .NET and Java platforms are the most sought-after general software development technology stacks. Microsoft .NET currently represents about 3.5% of all job openings, while Java is around 3% of all job openings. Initial research in 2010 from three of the top Computer Science programs in the United States, as reported by the GRE College Guide, shows that only a minimal number of classes ranging from program and development, Java, and C++ are offered as part of the program. The Computer Science and Information Technology programs must include introduction and advanced classes for both the Microsoft .NET and the Java platforms to meet the needs of the industry. Gartner, a renowned technology research company, showed the technology trends from 2006-2010 do not align with the technologies being taught as part of the Computer Science and Information Technology programs.

Other factors also contributed to the misalignment between the curriculum in the Computer Science and Information Technology programs and needs of the software development industry. The Computer Science and Information Technology industry is moving at a much faster pace than the pace of the curriculum updates in college and university Computer Science programs. The college and university professors are not adequately teaching the core fundamental and foundational programming principles required to maintain, design, and build web applications using the Enterprise Java platform or the Microsoft .NET platform. The skills and the experience of the college and university professors are not aligned properly with the technologies used in the industry.

It is evident after the problem documentation and literature review that the problem statement has supporting research and a major issue exists in the curriculum in the Computer Science and Information Technology programs. Research was completed to identify the gaps in the Computer Science and Information Technology programs.

Chapter 3: Outcome and Analysis

Goals and Expectations

The goals of this research project were to provide recommendations that need to be made to the Computer Science and Information Technology curriculum and improvements that can be made to hands-on labs, as it relates to maintaining, designing, and developing Enterprise class web applications. The research identified gaps between the existing curriculum and the software development industry. Resolving these gaps in college and university Computer Science and Information Technology programs will enable graduates to become better prepared for entry-level programming positions and be more proficient at maintaining, designing, and building simple N-tier Enterprise class web application. This action research project documented the specific recommendations required to improve our Computer Science and Information Technology bachelor and graduate programs.

The universities benefited in a number of ways from the results of this action research project. The universities will be more competitive with a modern and exciting Computer Science program that will be better aligned with the needs of the current software development industry. The universities curriculum, classes, and labs were also improved. The universities graduates benefited because they will be more competitive in the job marketplace and be better prepared for entry-level programming positions. The universities professors benefited because they discovered skills and technical gaps in their teachings required to improve their curriculum. And finally, the corporations hiring Computer Science and Information Technology graduates benefited because they can hire United States college graduates rather than filling these positions with lower cost offshore outsourcing resources from countries, such as India and China.

Expected Outcomes

The goals of the research were to identify specific changes that could be made to the curriculum to improve the skills in the areas in software development teams responsible for maintaining, designing, and building Enterprise web applications. These goals were achieved by aligning the curriculum of the classes closer to technology used in the industry, promoted more hands-on labs, and improved the readiness of the students for the industry. These additional classes will also improve

22

the attractiveness of the Computer Science program to potential future students to increase enrollment rates.

The research data from this project justified the recommendation of at least six additional hands-on labs that could be taken during the last two semesters of the Computer Science and Information Technology program. When a college or university implements the recommendations from this research their Computer Science or Information Technology program will differentiate their program from at least 80% of the top five University Computer Science programs in the United States.

Measurement of Outcomes

Both quantitative and qualitative research data was used in the action research project. Quantitative research data was obtained by analyzing the classes being offered in the current bachelor and graduate Computer Science and Information Technology programs from the top five universities in the United States. Resources for obtaining this research data and the analysis of the research data can be found in Appendix A. The technologies and skills being taught in the Computer Science and Information Technology programs were matched and compared against the essential technology training and skills required by the software development industry. To identify the technologies and skills required by the software development industry and quantify the readiness of the Computer Science and Information Technology graduate a series of two surveys and an interview were completed with the members of a software development team working in corporate America. The survey data provided concrete quantitative research data and the interview data provided the important qualitative research data. The survey and interview questions along with the research analysis can be found in Appendix B, Appendix C, and Appendix D.

The results of the university Computer Science and Information Technology program research along with the surveys and interviews were used to obtain research data that was used to identify curriculum gaps in the Computer Science and Information Technology programs. The results of the research were used to compare the current state of the Computer Science and Information Technology programs with the desired future state required by the software development industry. The analysis was used to identify gaps between the Computer Science and Information Technology curriculum, hands-on programming labs, and the technology training and skills required to design and build Enterprise class web applications in the software development industry.

Analysis of Results

An advanced Enterprise web application maintenance, design, and development program needs to be put in place by community colleges or universities Computer Science program. A search of the top bachelor and masters Computer Science programs showed that only introductory Enterprise web application programming classes are available for students.

As suggested by the Editorial Board of Software Development Times, a popular technical magazine that tracks current software development technologies and trends, they propose a new course for all Computer Science majors and that course would be of code maintenance (SD Editorial Board, 2010). A recent small survey was completed by the author with recent Computer Science and Information Technology graduates and found that these graduates had to obtain the required introductory industry knowledge either by working three to five years in the industry or by taking expensive certification classes. A bulk of this knowledge obtained after post-graduation can be taught today in our Computer Science and Information Technology programs. Advanced programming topics in the college catalog need to include the proper instruction on the design of N-Layer web applications along with industry best practices.

Chapter 4: Solution Strategy

Statement of Problem

The problem was that many college and university Computer Science graduates and Information Technology (IT) graduates are not properly prepared academically to maintain, design, and develop Enterprise class web applications. Computer Science graduates and Information Technology graduates must be properly trained to maintain and build web applications.

Discussion

The United States now has a shortage of IT and Computer Science skills (Bagaya, 2007). University administrators need to design undergraduate and graduate courses to attract new students and retain enrolled students (Bagaya, 2007). The current research shows that an issue in the United States is the declining enrollment rate of the Computer Science and Information Technology programs. Enrollment rates are declining in part because the programs are outdated, and administrators of universities need to design undergraduate courses to attract new students and retain enrolled students. Another contributing factor to the declining enrollment rates is the influence outsourcing United States programming positions to countries such as India and China. The United States must find creative approaches to improving the Computer Science and Information Technology programs, improve enrollment rates, and reduce the dependency on outsourced programming positions. Currently the Computer Science and Information Technology programs are not an attractive option for new students.

Web applications have become predominantly used to implement almost all current desktop, business, mobile, and personal applications. The technologies used to build web applications are even used as the foundation to build applications for consumer devices, such as advanced TV set top boxes and digital TV's. The Enterprise Java platform and the Microsoft .NET platform are the major platforms of choice for many companies who need to build these web applications. Research is required to determine how to improve the curriculum, how to improve the hands-on programming labs, and better prepare Computer Science and Information Technology graduates for entry into the current workforce for companies looking to hire software developers to design and develop web applications. Additionally, this research is important because if Computer Science graduates are not qualified to design and develop Enterprise class web applications, these programming positions will continue to be filled by using low-cost offshore outsource resources in countries, such as India and China.

Industry leaders and editors of industry trade journals have made a number of observations, expressed concerns, and made recommendations to improve Computer Science and Information Technology programs. One of the popular software industry journals is Software Development Times. This monthly journal tracks the trends, technologies, and corporations in the software development industry. Recently the Software Development Times editors asked: What are Computer Science students taught? New hire graduates are asked to write software and one of their first responsibilities includes code maintenance. Maintaining existing software is the quickest way to get up to speed, not only on the codebase itself but also on corporate coding practices. We propose a new course for all Computer Science majors. This course would be of code maintenance (SD Editorial Board, 2010). If one of the first responsibilities of new hire graduates of Computer Science and Information Technology programs is maintaining software, the skills required to maintain software must be properly taught in our colleges and universities.

More than 75% of job trends in 2011 demand the Enterprise Java platform or the Microsoft .NET platform. The Microsoft .NET and Java platforms are the most sought-after general software development technology stacks. Both the Microsoft .NET and Java platforms need to be included in Computer Science and the Information Technology programs to properly support the needs of the software industry.

The Computer Science and the Information Technology curriculum needs to be refreshed, updated, and aligned with the needs of the software industry. The Computer Science and the Information Technology curriculum will need to be updated to include a course on maintaining software. The Computer Science and the Information Technology curriculum will need to be updated to include an Enterprise web application-programming track. These tracks should be offered in either Enterprise Java or Microsoft .NET. The selection of the tracks should be provided as an option to the student. To complement the new web application-programming tracks the Computer Science curriculum will also need to include more hands-on programming labs that teach the student how to build N-tier Enterprise web applications using current technology, common design patterns, and industry standards. College and university professors also need to upgrade their skills and experience in the Enterprise Java platform and Microsoft .NET platform.

It was evident after the problem documentation and literature review that the problem statement has supporting research and a major issue exists in the curriculum in the Computer Science and Information Technology programs. Research was completed to identify the gaps in the Computer Science and Information Technology programs.

Selected Solutions

To identify the specific gaps in the Computer Science and Information Technology programs research data was collected using the following instruments:

1. A research of the top five major universities programs in Computer Science and Information Technology programs was completed. The research assembled an inventory of the technologies, standards, and platforms being taught in these programs. This inventory was compared and contrasted to the current technologies, standards, and platform trends used in the industry between 2005-2010 to build Enterprise web applications. The results of this research data and research data gathered during analysis were populated in a table outlined in Appendix A.

2. An anonymous survey was distributed to a current software development team in corporate America. The survey focused on determining the experience of the team in the core technical domains used to design and build Enterprise web applications. The survey was used to take inventory of the developer's skills and capabilities that they were taught to design and build Enterprise web applications as well as to use this inventory of skills to identify the potential gaps in the Computer Science and Information Technology programs. The questions for this survey and research data gathered during this survey are provided in Appendix B.

3. An anonymous survey was distributed to a current software development team in corporate America. The survey focused on determining the experience in the team on the basic skills required to maintain Enterprise web applications. The survey was used to take inventory of the developer's skills and capabilities that they were taught to maintain Enterprise web applications as well as to use this inventory of skills to identify the potential gaps in the Computer Science and Information Technology programs.

The questions for this survey and research data gathered during this survey are provided in Appendix C.

4. An interview was completed with five software developers in corporate America. The interview focused on the classes they received in a college or university Computer Science program and Information Technology program and how these classes related to the skills required for their first professional programming position. The interview also sought out recommendations from the recent college graduates on what could be done to improve university Computer Science program and Information Technology program. The questions for this interview and research data gathered during this interview are provided in Appendix D.

In addition to the above research the author gave a condensed 12-hour Web Application Design 101 course to a software development team. The course curriculum is outlined in Appendix E. After completing the web application design class, the students could model and design a web application leveraging either the Enterprise Java or the Microsoft .NET platforms. The students were introduced to industry best practices, technology frameworks, and learned a proven industry design methodology. Once the class was completed, the software development team was interviewed to see if the class would be appropriate for a Computer Science program. These interview questions were used to provide research data to identify any of the gaps in a Computer Science program or Information Technology program. The questions for this interview and research data gathered during this interview are provided in Appendix D.

The selected solutions were completed over a three-month timeline, required the writer and previously identified software development team as resources, and cost an estimated $25,000 to implement. The detailed implementation plan is included in Appendix F.

Chapter 5: Results and Recommendations

Results

The problem was that many college and university Computer Science graduates and Information Technology (IT) graduates are not properly prepared academically to maintain, design, and develop Enterprise class web applications. Computer Science graduates and Information Technology graduates must be properly trained to maintain and build web applications. The goals of the research were to identify specific changes that could be made to the curriculum to improve the skills in the areas in software development teams responsible for maintaining, designing, and building Enterprise web applications. Upon completion of the action research project at least six additional hands-on labs that could be taken during the last two semesters of the Computer Science and Information Technology program were recommended. When a college or university implements the recommendations from this research their Computer Science or Information Technology program will differentiate their program from at least 80% of the top five University Computer Science programs in the United States.

The instruments used to gather research data for the action research project consisted of analyzing the top five major universities Computer Science and Information Technology programs, conducting two surveys on the skills and technologies used to design, build, and maintain web applications, and conducting an interview with members of a software development team. The following paragraphs document the results of the research data and analysis that was conducted from the selected solutions.

The first research data gathered for analysis was to research the top five major universities Computer Science and Information Technology programs as identified from the GRE College Guide. The research data was completed to assemble an inventory of classes appropriate for web application design and development that were available from the top five university Computer Science and Information Technology programs in the United States. The top five universities analyzed were Stanford University, Massachusetts Institute of Technology, University of California – Berkeley, Carnegie Mellon University, and Cornell University. The research data from this analysis is documented in Appendix A. The following observations and gaps discovered from the analysis included:

- 100% of the universities taught a basic course in the Java programming language. However, none of the universities taught a class in the C# programming language used within the Microsoft .NET platform.
- 60% of the universities taught a basic web-programming course using the Enterprise Java platform. However, none of the universities taught the Microsoft .NET platform.
- 0% of the universities taught a course on software maintenance.
- 0% of the universities taught a course on the software development lifecycle (SDLC).
- 20% of the universities taught a course on web application design.
- 20% of the universities taught a course on building applications for a mobile platform.

Research data was gathered for analysis by conducting a survey with members of a software development team to identify gaps in skills required to design and build modern Enterprise web applications. The survey asked each software development team member to rate his or her experience in a number of technical areas using a Likert scale. The anonymous survey was conducted via e-mail. The research data from this analysis is documented in Appendix B. The following observations and gaps discovered from the analysis included:

- The team had very little knowledge in software architecture and software design.
- The team had good knowledge of the Microsoft .NET platform.
- The team had good knowledge of web technologies that included CSS, JavaScript, and AJAX.
- The team had very little knowledge of the MVC design pattern.
- The team had very little knowledge of web services and integration technologies.
- The team had good knowledge of database technologies that included SQL, ADO.NET, and PL/SQL.
- The team had very good knowledge of the C# programming language but had very little knowledge of the Java programming language.

Research data was gathered for analysis by conducting a survey with members of a software development team to identify gaps in skills required to maintain modern Enterprise web applications. The survey asked each software development team member to rate his or her experience in a number of technical areas using a Likert scale. The anonymous survey was conducted via e-mail using an online survey. The research data from this analysis is documented in Appendix C. The following observations and gaps discovered from the analysis included:

- A large majority (88%) of the population surveyed believed they learned the skills necessary to understand the SDLC process.
- A majority (67%) of the population surveyed did not learn how to apply requirements analysis when maintaining software.
- A large majority (55%-78%) of the population surveyed did not learn the skills to use the tools (debugger and profiler) required to maintain software (especially profiling).
- A majority (67%) of the population surveyed understood the concepts of a version control system.
- Over half of the population surveyed (56%) did not acquire the skills to add new features and document code required to maintain software.
- Almost half of the population surveyed (44%) did not acquire the skills required to give design and code reviews.
- A majority of the population surveyed (78%) believed they were prepared in college with the proper skills to enter the workforce to maintain software.

Research data was gathered for analysis by conducting an interview with members from a software development team to identify gaps in skills required to maintain modern Enterprise web applications. The population of the software development team included 20% community college graduates and 80% major state university graduates, 20% graduated during 1992-1998 and 80% graduated during 2001-2010, 40% received a BSCS, 40% received a BSCIS, and 20% received a BSET. A face-to-face interview was conducted with selected members of a software development team. The research data from this analysis is documented in Appendix D. The following observations and gaps discovered from the analysis included:

Internships should be mandatory. This might be difficult process to manage for companies. None of the technologies used in the internships were taught in school nor were the technologies ever mentioned (even in their senior year of college). This suggests that the Computer Science program was not aligned with the industry and was too far behind the industry.

- 100% of the interviewees maintained applications and 80% of the interviewees maintained web applications as part of their responsibilities of their first job after graduating from their program. However, none of the interviewees was taught the skills to maintain software in their college or university studies.
- The interviewees were taught basic object orientated skills, basic data structures, assembly language, Java, and database tables. Only one interviewee was taught .NET4.0 problem analysis, C#, and had the opportunity to take an introduction to web application design class that included HTML, CSS, JavaScript, AJAX, and XML.
- The interviewees' believed there was too much theory and not enough practical knowledge taught using real-world projects. Some classes such as artificial intelligence and compiler design were a waste of time and not relevant for their careers.
- The interviewees believe there was not enough practical knowledge taught on how to maintain software or the software development lifecycle (SDLC) process.
- The interviewees believe they should have been forced to use UML. One interviewee completed a web application class, but the class only introduced the student briefly to the MVC design pattern. The interviewees' believed there were too much theory and not enough coding. One interviewee was being taught the Pascal programming language when the industry was using C/C++.
- Some of the classes were taught online. The interviewee believed that an online classroom was not an effective environment to teach programming classes. Some classes even taught bad programming principles.
- 80% of the interviewees said their programs were simply outdated and not aligned with the skills that were required for their first programming position.
- 80% of the interviewees said their programs did not adequately prepare them to maintain, design, and program web applications. The programs were simply outdated and not aligned with the skills were required to maintain software. 60% of interviewees said that more hands-on labs are needed in the classroom.
- 100% of the interviewees said that the web application design class they were taught (in Appendix D) in their job should be added to the curriculum and taught in a Computer Science or Information Technology program.

- The interviewees made the following recommendations to improve the Computer Science and Information Technology programs:
  1. Minimize some of the elective classes (history, physiology, physics I and II, Calculus I, II, and III, Religions, etc.).
  2. More group projects need to be added to the program. The projects should be aligned to a real-world scenario and development process.
  3. Standardize on tools and use the same tools used in the industry. Leverage the free tools offered by Microsoft for the .NET platform.
  4. Teach the importance of code maintenance and performance.
  5. Teach more web application programming classes.
  6. Hire professors who have more real-world experience and are not outdated. Also bring industry experts into the classroom.
- The interviewees made the following recommendations to technology companies:
  1. Add more formal training programs.
  2. Promote the Microsoft Developer Network (MSDN).
  3. Offer tuition reimbursement programs.
  4. Be more proactive in internship programs.

The research data provided valuable insight into the curriculum of the current Computer Science and Information Technology programs. Valuable feedback was obtained from the survey data and interview data. This research data provided the information required to make specific recommendations to the Computer Science and Information Technology programs that could be used to easily improve the programs.

Discussion

The results of the research data and analysis clearly showed the top universities Computer Science and Information Technology programs in the United States are not aligned with the needs of the industry when preparing students to maintain, design, and build of web- applications. By far Stanford University provided the most progressive Computer Science program and even offered a mobile platform tracks that included classes in programming the iPhone and Android platforms. Ivan Kedrin from NY CTO, who is an online web technologist, reports that more than 75% of job trends in 2011 demand the Enterprise Java platform or the Microsoft .NET platform. The Microsoft .NET and Java platforms, as shown in figure 1, are the most sought-after general software development technology stacks. Currently, Microsoft .NET represents about 3.5% of all job openings, while Java is around 3% of all job openings. None of the top universities in the United States are even teaching the C# programming language or the Microsoft .NET platforms. None of the universities taught a course on software maintenance but yet this is one of the first primary responsibilities of a majority of Computer Science and Information Technology graduates. This gap must be resolved to properly prepare the graduates for their first job in the industry. None of the universities taught a course on the software development lifecycle (SDLC). This gap must be resolved to enable the graduates to properly understand the process used to design, build, test, and release software into the market. Web applications have become predominantly used to implement almost all current desktop, business, mobile, and personal applications. The technologies used to build web applications are even used as the foundation to build applications for consumer devices, such as advanced TV set top boxes and digital TV's. However, the research data showed that only 20% of the universities taught a course on web application design. These major gaps in the programs require the student or the industry to pick up the cost of training the student to fill in this major gap in the Computer Science and Information Technology program.

The surveys and interview conducted with the software development team yielded a number of surprising results. The interviewees' suggested that too much theory and not enough practical knowledge using real-world projects were taught in their programs. Some classes such as artificial intelligence and compiler design were a waste of time and not relevant for their careers. 80% of the interviewees said their programs were simply outdated and not aligned with the skills required for their first programming position. The programs were simply outdated and not aligned with the skills required to maintain software and 60% of interviewees said that more hands-on labs are needed in the classroom. The Computer Science and Information Technology program must be updated, refreshed, and aligned with the needs of the industry.

The research data from surveys and interview conducted with the software development team showed that there was not enough practical knowledge taught on how to maintain software or the software development lifecycle (SDLC) process. 100% of the interviewees indicated they were responsible for maintaining software applications. 80% of the interviewees' indicated they were responsible for maintaining web applications. However, none of the interviewees was taught the skills to maintain software in their college or university studies. A large majority

(55%-78%) of the population surveyed did not learn the skills to use the tools (debugger and profiler) required to maintain software. A majority (67%) of the population surveyed understood the concepts of a version control system. Over half of the population surveyed (56%) did not acquire the skills to add new features and document code required to maintain software. Almost half of the population surveyed (44%) did not acquire the skills required to give design and code reviews. These gaps must be resolved to properly prepare the graduates for their first job in the industry and prepare them to properly maintain software.

The research data from surveys and interview conducted with the software development team showed that the Computer Science and Information Technology programs lacked the proper classes in web application design and development. 80% of the interviewees said their programs did not adequately prepare them to maintain, design, and program web applications. 100% of the interviewees indicated that the web application design class they were taught (in Appendix D) should be added to the curriculum and taught in a Computer Science or Information Technology program.

Recommendations

After implementing the selected solutions and analyzing the research data obtained from research instruments a number of gaps were identified in the Computer Science or Information Technology programs. A summary of the gaps in the program included:

1. The C# programming language and the Microsoft .NET platform was not included in the program. A basic Microsoft .NET platform class and also an advanced Microsoft .NET platform class must be added to the program.
2. The program only included classes on the basic Java EE platform. An advanced Java EE platform class must be added to the program.
3. The program did not include a class to introduce the Software Development Lifecycle (SDLC) process. A SDLC process class must be added to the program.
4. The program did not include a class on software maintenance. A software maintenance class must be added to the program.
5. The program did not include a class on general web application design. A general web application design class that includes fundamentals on N-Layered design, Unified Modeling Language (UML), requirements analysis, industry

best practices, and industry design patterns must be added to the program.

To resolve the gaps identified during the analysis of the research data the following recommendations are being made to the Computer Science and Information Technology programs.

	Curriculum Recommendation	Curriculum Description
1	Web Application Design Class	This class would be a platform neutral class that teaches the fundamentals on N-Layered design, Unified Modeling Language (UML), requirements analysis, industry best practices, and industry design patterns. The class would also include an introduction to the Software Development Lifecycle (SDLC) process. The class would include hands-on programming labs that include requirements decomposition using a real-world business scenario and using Unified Modeling Language (UML) to model a software design. See Appendix D for course details.
2	Web Application Programming Track	This programming track would be offered to students as part of a focused web application design and development track. The student would have the option to take either classes targeted to the Microsoft .NET Platform or the Enterprise Java Platform.
2a	Web Application Foundation	This class would teach the fundamentals and technologies used to build web applications. Technologies taught would include basic HTML, Cascading Style Sheets (CSS), JavaScript, and the HTTP protocol. This class would include hands-on programming labs that would build a static website using HTML, CSS, and JavaScript.

2b	Microsoft .NET Platform	This class would teach the student how to design and build dynamic web applications using the Microsoft .NET Platform. Fundamentals including ASP.NET, Windows Communication Foundation, Windows Work Flow, and Entity Framework will be taught as part of this class. Labs in the class would apply the fundamentals and learning objective taught as part of the Web Application Design Class. The hands-on programming labs included as part of this class would consist of modeling a software design using a real-world business scenario and exercise each phase of the Software Development Lifecycle (SDLC) process.
2c	Enterprise Java Platform	This class would teach the student how to design and build dynamic web applications using the Enterprise Java Platform. Fundamentals including Servlets, JavaServer Faces, Enterprise Java Beans, and Java Persistence Framework will be taught as part of this class. Labs in the class would apply the fundamentals and learning objective taught as part of the Web Application Design Class. The hands-on programming labs included as part of this class would consist of modeling a software design using a real-world business scenario and exercise each phase of the Software Development Lifecycle (SDLC) process.

5	Maintaining Software Class	This class would teach the fundamentals for how to maintain software. Fundamentals taught would include using a software debugger, using a performance profiler, version control system, commenting code, and peer code reviews. The hands-on programming labs included as part of this class would consist of optimizing a piece of software, adding appropriate comments to the code, and giving a peer code review.

The general recommendations from the members of the software development team should also be considered. Computer Science and Information Technology administrators should minimize some of the elective classes (history, physiology, physics I and II, Calculus I, II, and III, Religions, etc.), add more group projects, and align the projects with a real-world scenario and development process. Just as important is to ensure that administrators hire professors who have more real-world experience and are not outdated.

A hiring manager made the following quote. "I have never interviewed a candidate right out of college who I would hire. No recent graduate that I have interviewed has had sufficient understanding of real-world problems to be useful to me, at least for the salary that the interviewees were expecting" (Ward, 2010, p. 1). The before mentioned quote from a hiring manager in the industry should be motivation enough for college and university Computer Science and Information Technology administrators to take notice in the effectiveness of his or her programs.

Research to improve our Computer Science and Information Technology programs should not stop here. The United States must find new and creative approaches as well as fund additional research to improve the Computer Science and Information Technology programs, improve enrollment rates, and reduce the dependency on outsourced programming positions. Currently the Computer Science and Information Technology programs are not an attractive option for new students. Implementing the recommendations and improvements to the curriculum as suggested in this research will result in improving 100% of the top five universities identified in this research. Implementing the recommendations and improvements as suggested in this research will result in a Computer Science and the Information Technology curriculum that will be refreshed, updated, and aligned with the needs of the software industry.

Solutions for
My Action Research Project
Six Years Later

Chapter 6: Solving My Research Problem

Academic Progress Six Years Later

This chapter summarizes how Grand Canyon University (GCU), a major U.S. University located in Phoenix Arizona, and their "state of the art" College of Science in Engineering and Technology programs, and more specifically the programs that are part of the Technology college, have actually solved many of the issues discovered from the research that I completed six years ago. It should be noted that I am currently a full-time faculty member and program lead at GCU for the Bachelor of Science in Computer Programming (BSCP) program, which is one of the major programs within the College of Technology. It should also be noted that when I originally complete my research six years ago, I was still actively working in the industry and had no affiliation with GCU.

The Bachelor of Science in Computer Programming degree at Grand Canyon University is like no other program in the country in that its emphasis is entirely on software development. This program blends a perfect combination of theory and practical application where students learn four programming languages and four web application frameworks along with obtaining a superb foundation in algorithms & data structures, operating system concepts, cloud computing, business, and project management. During the program, students design solutions to problems using a formal design specification, author test plans, and develop 8 to 10 mobile and web applications individually and in small teams. Finally, in their senior year, the students finish the program with a yearlong capstone project where they exercise all the phases within the SDLC lifecycle.

This chapter provides a summary of issues, gaps, and recommendations from my original research six years ago, which are then aligned to how GCU and their Technology programs in Computer Programming, Computer Science, and Information Technology have solved my research problem.

The following table summarizes the curriculum recommendations I made six years ago as a result of my research and how GCU has met those recommendations.

	Original Curriculum Recommendation From 2012	Original Curriculum Recommendation Description	How GCU Solves this Problem Today
1	**Web Application Design Class**	This class would be a platform neutral class that teaches the fundamentals on N-Layered design, Unified Modeling Language (UML), requirements analysis, industry best practices, and industry design patterns. The class would also include an introduction to the Software Development Lifecycle (SDLC) process.	GCU has a number of classes dedicated to helping solve this problem. One class, which is part of the Bachelor of Science in Computer Programming (BSCP) program, is Written and Verbal Communication for Software Development. This classes teaches the fundamentals of the Software Development Lifecycle (SDLC) process.
		The class would include hands-on programming labs that include requirements decomposition using a real-world business scenario and using Unified Modeling Language	This class also teaches the fundamentals of project management using a variety of delivery methodologies, including Agile Scrum.

		(UML) to model a software design.	The BSCP program is a unique program that focuses on software development. In this program students learn a number of programming languages and web frameworks, along with foundational classes, such as operating systems and cloud computing. All technical classes are project-based where students deliver formal design specifications that include a number of UML diagram types that includes UML class diagrams.
2	**Web Application Programming Track**	This programming track would be offered to students as part of a focused web application design and development track. The student would have the option to take either classes targeted to the Microsoft .NET Platform or the Enterprise Java Platform.	The BSCP program is a unique program that focuses on software development. In this program students learn a number of programming languages (Java, C#, PHP, and JavaScript) as well as a number of web frameworks (Enterprise Java, Spring MVC, .NET

			MVC, PHP Laravel, and Angular, React, Express in JavaScript), along with foundational classes, such as operating systems and cloud computing, where students deploy applications to all the major cloud platforms.
2a	Web Application Foundation	This class would teach the fundamentals and technologies used to build web applications. Technologies taught would include basic HTML, Cascading Style Sheets (CSS), JavaScript, and the HTTP protocol. This class would include hands-on programming labs that would build a static website using HTML, CSS, and JavaScript.	The BSCP program is a unique program that focuses on software development. In the program students learn a number of web frameworks (Enterprise Java, Spring MVC, .NET MVC, PHP Laravel, and Angular, React, Express in JavaScript), which requires the students to learn and apply HTML, CSS, jQuery, and Bootstrap in the design and implementation of their web applications.
2b	Microsoft .NET Platform	This class would teach the student how to design and build dynamic web	The BSCP program is a unique program that focuses on software

		applications using the Microsoft .NET Platform. Fundamentals including ASP.NET, Windows Communication Foundation, Windows Work Flow, and Entity Framework will be taught as part of this class. Labs in the class would apply the fundamentals and learning objective taught as part of the Web Application Design Class. The hands-on programming labs included as part of this class would consist of modeling a software design using a real-world business scenario and exercise each phase of the Software Development Lifecycle (SDLC) process.	development. In the program students learn a number of web frameworks, one of which is .NET MVC. GCU is a teaching university using a project-based learning strategy in all of the class designs. Students design applications using a formal design specification. By the time they reach their senior year and their Capstone Project, they will have designed and implemented 8-10 applications individually or in teams. Seniors spend two semesters completing their Capstone Project where they exercise the full Software Development Lifecycle (SDLC) process by delivering a Project Proposal, Functional Requirements specification, Technical Design specification, Test Plans, and

			application code.
2c	Enterprise Java Platform	This class would teach the student how to design and build dynamic web applications using the Enterprise Java Platform. Fundamentals including Servlets, JavaServer Faces, Enterprise Java Beans, and Java Persistence Framework will be taught as part of this class. Labs in the class would apply the fundamentals and learning objective taught as part of the Web Application Design Class. The hands-on programming labs included as part of this class would consist of modeling a software design using a real-world business scenario and exercise each phase of the Software Development Lifecycle (SDLC) process.	The BSCP program is a unique program that focuses on software development. In the program students learn a number of web frameworks, which includes the Enterprise Java platform and also the Spring Framework. These web frameworks are part of a five course Java sequence of classes provided to the students as part of the standard BSCP program.
3	**Maintaining Software Class**	This class would teach the	GCU faculty is evaluating courses

		fundamentals for how to maintain software. Fundamentals taught would include using a software debugger, using a performance profiler, version control system, commenting code, and peer code reviews. The hands-on programming labs included as part of this class would consist of optimizing a piece of software, adding appropriate comments to the code, and giving a peer code review.	in the BSCP program that will fully resolve this problem. The students do have an individual hands-on activity in a number of classes where they use the debugger. All programming classes require that students maintain their code in a source code repository. Additional work needs to be done to add more activities related to peer code reviews and software maintenance best practices.

The following table summarizes the program recommendations made by the research candidates that were discovered six years ago during my research and how GCU has met those recommendations.

	Original Program Recommendation From 2012	Original Program Recommendation Description	How GCU Solves the Problem Today
1	Minimize some of the elective classes	The research candidates felt their program had too much theory and some of the elective classes were not	Although some programs in the Technology college are driven by requirements established by accreditation

		beneficial	bodies, GCU has other programs, such as the BSCP program, that focuses less on math, science, and theory. The BSCP program is ideal for students who desire a program with less theory and more of a practical hands-on focus.
2	More group projects need to be added to the program	The research candidates felt their program did not have enough hands-on activities and projects	GCU is a teaching university with a project-based learning strategy. Many of the projects completed by students are completed in a small team.
3	Standardize on tools and use the same tools used in the industry	The research candidates felt their program felt they were not using the same tools as being using in the industry	GCU's programs in the Technology college are all aligned to industry needs using tools and technologies required by the industry.
4	Teach the importance of code maintenance and performance	The research candidates felt their program were not trained with skills that were required on their first job after graduating, which is	GCU faculty is evaluating courses in the BSCP program that will help address this gap. Additional work needs to be done to add more

		maintaining code	activities related to peer code reviews and software maintenance best practices.
5	Teach more web application programming classes	The research candidates felt their program did not include a broad or deep enough focus on web application frameworks	The BSCP program provides the students with the experience using a number of web frameworks (Enterprise Java, Spring MVC, .NET MVC, PHP Laravel, and Angular/React/Express in JavaScript). The BSCS program has also been enhanced to not only just teach C++ but also adds the Java programming language to the program.
6	Hire professors who have more real-world experience and are not outdated. Also bring industry experts into the classroom	The research candidates felt their program felt many of their instructors were out of date and did not bring enough real-world expertise into the classroom	A large majority of the faculty in the GCU Technology college have 15+ years of industry experience.

The following table summarizes the program and curriculum gaps that were discovered six years ago in my research and how GCU has closed those gaps.

	Original Gap From 2012	Original Gap Description	How GCU Solves the Gap Today
1	Internships should be mandatory	The research candidates felt that companies needed to be more involved with students and provide a comprehensive internship program	The Technology college has dedicated personnel who work with companies and industry leaders to place students in internship programs.
2	Need more knowledge in software architecture and software design	The research candidates felt their program did not provide enough practical knowledge in their program or enough knowledge in software design	GCU is a teaching university with a project-based learning strategy. Many of the classes in the BSCP program have students deliver formal design specifications with their projects, apply design patterns in their solutions, and practice industry best practices.
3	Need more knowledge in design patterns	The research candidates felt their program did not provide enough practical knowledge in common design patterns used to build enterprise class applications	The BSCP program has a dedicated class in design patterns. As part of the web framework classes, instructors teach a number of common design patterns including the MVC, Facade, DAO, and

			DTO patterns.
4	Need more knowledge of web services and integration technologies	The research candidates felt their program did not provide enough practical knowledge in web service technologies and technologies used to integrate applications and systems together	A number of the web framework classes within the BSCP program teach the technologies that support REST API's and Messaging API's along with the theory of SOAP based API's.
5	Need to learn how to apply requirements analysis when maintaining software	The research candidates felt their program did not provide enough practical knowledge in how to consume requirements and build solutions to meet those requirements	GCU is a teaching university with a project-based learning strategy. All project assignments are written in terms of functional and technical requirements that the students consume and design their solution against.
6	Need to learn the skills to use the tools (debugger and profiler) required to maintain software	The research candidates felt their program did not provide enough practical knowledge or hands on experience using a debugger and profile, which are commonly used when maintaining software	Many of the programming language and web framework classes within the BSCP program have assessed activities that measure whether students learned how to use the debugger.
7	Need to acquire the skills to add new features and document	The research candidates felt their program did not provide enough	Many of the programming language and web framework classes

	code required to maintain software	practical knowledge and skills required to maintain software	within the BSCP program have rubrics, which measure the student's ability to write commented and maintainable code.
8	Need to acquire the skills required to give design and code reviews	The research candidates felt their program did not provide enough practical knowledge and skills required to perform peer code and design reviews	GCU faculty is evaluating courses in the BSCP program that will help address this gap. Additional work needs to be done to add more activities related to peer code reviews.
9	Need knowledge in more than a single programming language and web stack framework	The research candidates felt their program did not provide enough knowledge on multiple programming languages and web frameworks	The BSCP program teaches the students a number of programming languages (Java, C#, PHP, and JavaScript) as well a number of web frameworks (Enterprise Java, Spring MVC, .NET MVC, PHP Laravel, and Angular, React, Express in JavaScript). The BSCS program has also been enhanced to not only teach C++ but also adds the Java programming language to the program.
10	Need less theory and	The research candidates felt their	GCU is a teaching university with a

	more practical knowledge taught using real-world projects	program did not provide enough practical knowledge, was too theory based, and without enough hands-on projects	project-based learning strategy. Many of the classes in the Technology programs have students deliver solutions and working applications as part of their projects.
11	Need to avoid classes such as artificial intelligence and compiler design, which were a waste of time and not relevant for their careers	The research candidates felt their program had too many classes without a practical application or relevance to their careers	GCU faculty is evaluating processes to help address this gap and by having instructors ensure they clearly articulate to the students the value, relevance, and practical application of the learning objectives of their classes they are taking.
12	Need to avoid teaching technical classes online	The research candidates felt their program being taught online was not an effective modality and was not an effective environment to teach programming classes	Currently many of the Science and Engineering classes at GCU are not taught online. GCU will run their Technology programs once they can be effectively run online while staying true to the goals of hands-on project-based learning strategies used in many of the classes.
13	Programs need to be kept up to date and aligned with the skills	The research candidates felt their program was outdated and not aligned to the	GCU staffs its own Content Design and Delivery team, is very supportive of faculty

students needed for their first programming position	needs and skills required by the industry	when it comes to making minor course revisions, and every 3-5 years all programs have the opportunity to go through a major program revision. This keeps the GCU programs fresh, relevant, and aligned to the industry.
		GCU also has industry leaders on their Technology Advisory Boards to help ensure programs stay aligned to industry needs.

State of the Industry Six Years Later

The technology field is always evolving and changing. Leaders in the industry often introduce new programming languages, frameworks, and methodologies to solve new and more complex problems. The following tables provide a brief snapshot of the programming languages and frameworks currently used and in demand illustrating how GCU's Technology programs in Computer Programming, Computer Science, and Information Technology aligns to those needs.

The following table outlines data published in 2018 from IEEE Spectrum summarizing the top Web Development Programming Languages used in the industry.

Technology	Rank by IEEE	Rank by Jobs	How GCU Solves the Gap Today
Java	3 out 48	2 out 48	Currently taught in the BSCP program
C#	5 out 48	5 out 48	Currently taught in the BSCP program
PHP	6 out 48	8 out 48	Currently taught in the BSCP program
JavaScript	8 out 48	6 out 48	Planned to be taught in the BSCP program

The following table outlines data published in 2019 from Stack Overflow summarizing the most popular Programming and Scripting Technologies used in the industry.

Technology	Rank	How GCU Solves the Gap Today
JavaScript	1	Planned to be taught in the BSCP program
HTML/CSS	2	Currently taught in the BSCP program
SQL	3	Currently taught in the BSCP program
Python	4	Currently taught in the BSCP program
Java	5	Currently taught in the BSCP program
Bash	6	Currently taught in the BSCP program
C#	7	Currently taught in the BSCP program
PHP	8	Currently taught in the BSCP program
C++	9	Currently taught in the BSCS and BSEE programs
Typescript	10	Planned to be taught in the BSCP program

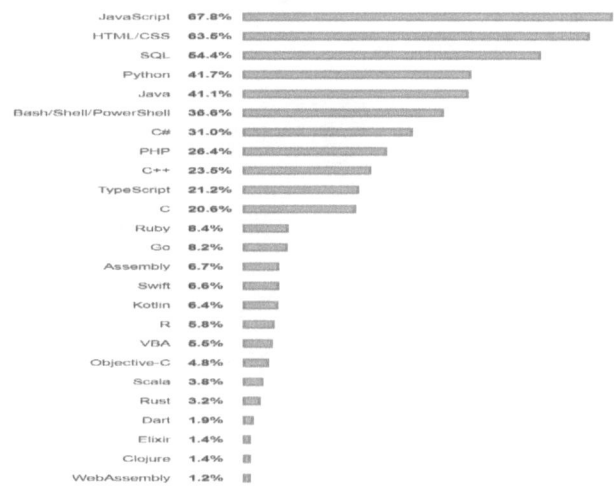

The following table outlines data published in 2019 from TIOBE summarizing the most popular Programming Languages used in the industry.

Technology	Rank	How GCU Solves the Gap Today
Java	1	Currently taught in the BSCP program
C	2	Planned to be taught in the BSCP program
C++	3	Currently taught in the BSCS and BSEE programs
Python	4	Currently taught in the BSCS and BSIT programs
Visual Basic .NET	6	Currently not taught in any program
C#	5	Currently taught in the BSCP program
JavaScript	8	Planned to be taught in the BSCP program
SQL	9	Currently taught in the BSCP program
PHP	7	Currently taught in the BSCP program
Assembly Language	13	Currently taught in the BSCS, BSIT, and BSEE programs

The following table outlines data published in 2019 from Stack Overflow summarizing the most popular Web Frameworks used in the industry.

Technology	Rank	How GCU Solves the Gap Today
React.js	1	Planned to be taught in the BSCP program
Angular/Angular.js	2	Planned to be taught in the BSCP program
ASP.NET	3	Currently taught in the BSCP program
Express	4	Planned to be taught in the BSCP program
Spring	5	Currently taught in the BSCP program
Vue.js	6	Currently not taught in any program
Django	7	Currently not taught in any program
Flask	8	Currently not taught in any program
Laravel	9	Currently taught in the BSCP program
Ruby on Rails	10	Currently not taught in any program
Drupal	11	Planned to be taught in the BSCP program

Node.js	49.6%
Angular	36.9%
React	27.8%
.NET Core	27.2%
Spring	17.6%
Django	13.0%
Cordova	8.5%
TensorFlow	7.8%
Xamarin	7.4%
Spark	4.8%
Hadoop	4.7%
Torch/PyTorch	1.7%

Chapter 7: Closing Thoughts

Six years ago, and discussed in chapters 1 thru 5, and through a research project, I made the following observations and recommendations regarding the Computer Science and Information Technology programs in the United States:

- The United States must find new and creative approaches as well as fund additional research to improve the Computer Science and Information Technology programs, improve enrollment rates, and reduce the dependency on outsourced programming positions.

- Currently the Computer Science and Information Technology programs are not an attractive option for new students. Implementing the recommendations and improvements to the curriculum as suggested from this research (from 2010) will result in improving 100% of the universities identified in this research paper.

- Implementing the recommendations and improvements as suggested from this research (from 2010) will result in a Computer Science and the Information Technology curriculum that will be refreshed, updated, and aligned with the needs of the software industry.

In a short period of time, six years to be exact, universities and companies across the United States have made great strides and made wonderful progress to help solve my research problem I identified in 2010. Today universities are now offering more elective classes and emphases giving students more options and flexibility in the technical programs they choose. Companies are also being more proactive in establishing formal internship programs, partnering with local universities, and giving students the opportunity for year around internship jobs that often lead to full time positions after graduation.

I believe I can safely and proudly state that Grand Canyon University, with its focus as a teaching university and project-based learning strategy, have truly made phenomenal strides in helping to solve my research problem. Kudos to the leaders at Grand Canyon University for the vision and foresight that actually helped solve the research problem I identified six years ago.

References

ACM. (2011). *Association for Computing Machinery*.
    Retrieved from http://www.acm.org/.

Bagaya, Martin H.. (2007). *An Analysis of IT/IS Offshore Outsourcing:*
    Educator Perspectives. Nova Southeastern University. 2007.
    Retrieved June 27, 2009 from ProQuest database.

Ensynch Corporation. (2011). *Ensynch Home Page*.
    Retrieved July1, 2011 from http://www.ensynch.com.

GRE Guide. (2009, June 27). *GRE College Guide*.
    Retrieved June 27, 2009 from
    http://www.greguide.com/comps.html.

Hoganson, K. (2004). *Computer Science Curricula In A Global Competitive*
    Environment. Consortium for Computing Sciences in Colleges.
    Retrieved June 1, 2011 from ProQuest database.

IEEE. (2011). *IEEE - The world's largest professional association for the*
    advancement of technology.
    Retrieved from http://www.ieee.org/.

Sun Microsystems Classes. (2009). *Java Programming Training*.
    Retrieved June 27, 2009 from
    http://www.exitcertified.com/training-class/java-training-sun-
    microsystems.html.

Kedrin, Ivan. (2011). *NY CTO: Web Application Development Technology*
    Demand Trends & Predictions.
    Retrieved July 7, 2011 from
    http://nyccto.wordpress.com/2010/04/19/web-application-
    development-technology-demand-trends-predictions.

LangPop.com. (2001). *Programming Language Popularity*.
    Retrieved July 1, 2011 from http://langpop.com/.

Lewis, B. (May 2010). *The Sad Standards of Computer-related College Degrees*.
　　　Retrieved from http://www.infoworld.com/d/adventures-in-
　　　it/the-sad-standards-computer-related-college-degrees-202.

Maglitta, Joseph. (1996). *IS schools: Need improvement*. Computerworld.
　　　Framingham.
　　　Retrieved June 27, 2009 from ProQuest database.

Microsoft Corporation. (2011). *Microsoft .NET Framework*.
　　　Retrieved July 1, 2011 from http://www.microsoft.com/net/.

Microsoft Corporation. (2011). *MSDN*.
　　　Retrieved July 1, 2011 from http://msdn.microsoft.com.

Needleman, Sarah E. (2007). *What Major '07 Headlines Say About '08 Job
　　　Market; Alternative Energy, Web Developing, Risk Analysis Are Hot;
　　　Airlines, Home Lending Are Not*. Wall Street Journal. (Eastern
　　　edition). New York, N.Y.: Dec 11, 2007. pg. B.12
　　　Retrieved June 27, 2009 from ProQuest database.

Oracle. (2011). *Java EE At a Glance*.
　　　Retrieved July 1, 2011 from
　　　http://www.oracle.com/technetwork/java/javaee/overview/.

Oracle. (2011). *Java Training Course Catalog*.
　　　Retrieved June 27, 2009 from http://education.oracle.com.

Schindler, Esther. (2005). *The Truth for Computer Science Grads*.
　　　Retrieved July 9, 2011 from Software Development Times
　　　http://www.union.edu/N/DS/s.php?s=5588.

SD Times Editorial Board. (2010). *Let's Teach Maintenance*.
　　　Retrieved April 15, 2010 from
　　　http://www.sdtimes.com/SearchResult/34244.

Simmons, Chris B. & Simmons Lakisha L.. (2010). *Gaps in the computer
　　　science curriculum: an exploratory study of industry professionals. Journal of
　　　Computing Sciences in Colleges*, 25(5).
　　　Retrieved June 1, 2011 from ACM Digital Library at
　　　http://portal.acm.org.

Technology Research – Gartner Inc. (n.d.).
Retrieved July 9, 2011 from Online web site:
http://www.gartner.com.

U.S. News and World Report. (2009, June 27). *Best Graduate Schools.*
Retrieved June 27, 2009 from
http://grad-schools.usnews.rankingsandreviews.com/best-
graduate-schools.

MSDN Magazine. Ward, K. (2010, July). *Over-Educated, Yet Under-
Qualified?.*
Retrieved from
http://msdn.microsoft.com/en-us/magazine/ff797912.aspx.

IEEE Spectrum (2018). *Top Programming Languages.*
Retrieved June 1, 2019 from https://spectrum.ieee.org.

Stack Overflow (2019). *Top Programming and Scripting Technologies.*
Retrieved June 1, 2019 from
https://insights.stackoverflow.com/survey/2019.

TIOBE (2019). *The Most popular Programming Languages.*
Retrieved June 1, 2019 from
https://www.tiobe.com/tiobe-index/.

Grand Canyon University (2019). *GCU Programs Home Page.*
Retrieved June 1, 2019 from
https://www.gcu.edu/degree-programs/

Reha, M. K. (2011). *Online Portfolio – Master's Degree Program.*
Retrieved from http://www.ontheedgesc.com/masters/.

Appendix A: Research Data - University Computer Science Program Analysis

The following research data was completed to assemble an inventory of classes appropriate for web application design and development. These classes were offered at the top five University Computer Science and Information Technology programs in the United States.

Web Application Design, Mobile Technology, and Web Application Development Classes Available	Gaps/Notes
Stanford University Analysis	
Core BSCS classes taught: 1. Computer Organization and Systems: C programming language down to the microprocessor. 2. Object-Oriented Systems Design: Intermediate Java and Java Swing. How the web works with Servlets, and JSP on Tomcat using Subversion. 3. Introduction to Databases: XML, SQL, some UML, constraints, views, triggers, and even NoSQL.	Gaps: 1. No .NET was taught. Need basic .NET class and also an advanced .NET class. 2. Only the basic Java EE was taught. Need an advanced Java EE class. 3. Need SDLC process class. 4. Need Software Maintenance class. 5. Need general Web Application Design class. Notes: 1. The most progressive Computer Science program in the top 5 universities. Even had both iPhone and Android programming tracks.
4. HCI Technology	

Laboratory: HTML, intro to CSS, PHP, JavaScript, jQuery, and even jQTouch. 5. iPhone Application Programming. 6. Android Programming. 7. Cloud Commuting. 8. Senior Project, a number of Independent Projects, and Database Project.	

Massachusetts Institute of Technology Analysis	
Core EECS classes taught: 1. Elements of Software Construction. 2. Create Video Games..	Gaps: 1. No .NET was taught. Need basic .NET class and also an advanced .NET class. 2. Only the basic Java EE was taught. Need an advanced Java EE class. 3. Need SDLC process class. 4. Need Software Maintenance class. 5. Need general Web Application Design class. 6. No mobile programming track. Notes: 1. Lots of theory and was very engineering centric.

University of California - Berkeley Analysis	
Core EECS classes taught: 1. JAVA for Programmers and Data Structures.	Gaps: 1. No .NET was taught. Need basic .NET class and also an advanced .NET class.

2. Introduction to Database Systems.	2. No Java EE was taught. Need basic Java EE class and also an advanced Java EE class. 3. Need SDLC process class. 4. Need Software Maintenance class. 5. Need general Web Application Design class. 6. No mobile programming track. Notes: 1. Lots of theory and was very engineering centric.
Carnegie Mellon University Analysis	
Core BSCS classes taught: 1. Effective Programming in C and UNIX. 2. Database Applications: SQL. 3. Bug Catching: Automated Program Verification and Testing. 4. Fundamental Data Structures. 5. Foundations of Programming Languages. 6. Introduction to Computer and Network Security and Applied Cryptography. 7. Introduction to Computer Security. 8. Fault-Tolerant Distributed Systems. 9. Internet Services.	Gaps: 1. No .NET was taught. Need basic .NET class and also an advanced .NET class. 2. No Java EE was taught. Need basic Java EE class and also an advanced Java EE class. 3. Need SDLC process class. 4. Need Software Maintenance class. 5. Need general Web Application Design class. 6. No mobile programming track. Notes: 1. Lots of theory and was very engineering centric.

Cornell University Analysis	
Core BSCS classes taught: 1. Introduction to Computing Using Java. 2. Transition to Object-Oriented Programming (using Java). 3. Introductory Design and Programming for the Web (XHTML, CSS, and PHP). 4. Introduction to Mobile Application Development. 5. Object-Oriented Programming and Data Structures (in Java or C++). 6. Intermediate Design and Programming for the Web (PHP, MySQL, JavaScript, AJAX). 7. Web Information Systems (XML, XSLT). 8. Introduction to Database Systems (XML, XQUery). 9. The Architecture of Large-Scale Information Systems (N-Tier, Web Services, .NET, Java EE).	**Gaps:** 1. 1 class on N-Tier web applications and mentioned web services, .NET, and Java EE. 2. Need SDLC process class. 3. Need Software Maintenance class. 4. Need general Web Application Design class. 5. No mobile programming track. **Notes:** 1. Lots of theory and was very engineering centric. 2. The 2nd most progressive Computer Science program behind Stanford.

Appendix B: Research Data - Survey Questions, Core Web Application Design and Development Skills

The following technical areas were studied using a survey that was used to obtain research data from a software development team to identify gaps in skills required to design and build modern Enterprise web applications. The survey asked each software development team member to rate his or her experience in each of the technical areas using a Likert scale. The survey was conducted via e-mail using the following instructions.

Step 1: Please fill out each of the technologies in each of the domains listed and provide an assessment of your experience and understanding of the technology. Use the following Likert Scale to rank your skills:

> 1 – no knowledge at all or never heard of the technology
> 2 – very little knowledge (I know what the technology is but have no book or practical knowledge)
> 3 – some knowledge (I have some book knowledge but no practical knowledge)
> 4 – good knowledge (I have practical industry knowledge)
> 5 – expert (expert knowledge, mentor ability)

Step 2: Indicate (with a Y or N) in the far-right column whether the associated technology domain is of interest to you for future projects or training.

Technology Domain	Skills Assessment? (1 none to 5 expert)	Future Interest? (Yes or No)
Architecture and Design		
Enterprise Architect	2.18	80%
Solution Architect	2.45	80%
Applications Architect	2.73	90%
Security Architect	2.09	90%
Integration Architect	2.27	90%
UML (Software Modeling)	2.91	80%
Design Patterns	3.00	90%

Reference Implementation	1.80	80%
Held Design Reviews	2.82	70%
Held Code Reviews	2.82	70%
Authored Standards	2.45	70%
Authored Best Practices	2.36	70%
.NET Presentation		
Classic ASP	3.18	20%
ASP .NET3.5 (or later)	3.36	80%
.NET MVC	2.09	70%
.NET AJAX	2.82	60%
CSS	3.36	70%
JavaScript	3.27	70%
JSON	1.91	60%
XSLT	2.55	50%
jQuery	1.64	50%
Prototype.js	1.36	50%
.NET Services/Integration		
.NET WCF	2.82	70%
.NET WWF	2.73	60%
.NET Unity Framework	2.09	60%
C# Business Services	1.18	70%
SOAP Web Services	1.55	80%
REST Web Services	1.91	70%
Messaging (MS MQ, MQ)	1.27	70%
Rules Engine	1.18	70%
ETL Framework/Server	1.36	70%
.NET Data Access		
.NET ADO	3.00	60%
LINQ	1.82	70%
nHibernate (or other ORM)	1.45	70%
PL/SQL	4.00	80%
SQL	4.00	80%
Security		
Authentication	3.36	70%
Authorization (Roles, etc.)	2.27	70%

LDAP	2.27	70%
SAML	1.09	60%
Kerberos	1.18	50%
SSL	2.73	70%
PCI Standard	1.36	60%
OWASP	1.00	40%
Web SSO (SiteMinder, etc.)	1.00	40%
SOA		
XML	3.00	60%
XSD	3.00	60%
WS-* Web Service Standards	1.00	80%
ESB	1.00	50%
BPEL/BPEL Engine	1.00	40%
Languages		
C#	3.82	60%
Java	2.73	100%
Perl	1.91	60%
F#	1.55	40%
Scala	1.36	40%

Appendix C: Research Data - Survey Questions, Maintaining Software Skills and Tools

The following survey questions were used to obtain research data from a software development team to identify gaps in skills required to maintain modern Enterprise web applications. The survey asked each software development team member to rate his or her experience in each of the technical areas using a Likert scale. The survey was conducted via an online survey.

1. I was taught the fundamentals of the processes involved in the Software Development Life Cycle.
2. I studied an existing software program and was taught how to add new features to it.
3. I was taught how to document business requirements for new features that could be added to an existing software program.
4. I was taught how to update existing software code documentation for existing software programs so my peers could easily maintain them.
5. I was taught how to use an IDE debugger for the Java, C#, or C/C++ programming languages.
6. I was taught how to use an IDE performance profiler for the Java, C#, or C/C++ programming languages.
7. I was taught the fundamentals of how to prepare, communicate, and deliver a design review with my peers.
8. I was taught the fundamentals of how to prepare, communicate, and deliver a code review with my peers.
9. I was taught the fundamentals for how to use a version control system.
10. I was prepared with the appropriate software development skills in college so once I started to work professionally as a software developer, I could maintain existing software programs.

I learned the required Software Development Processes?				
	Strongly Agree	Agree	Disagree	Strongly Disagree
SDLC Process	44%	44%	11%	0%
Requirements Analysis	11%	22%	56%	11%

I learned the required skills for the programming tools?				
	Strongly Agree	Agree	Disagree	Strongly Disagree
IDE Debugger	11%	33%	33%	22%
IDE Profiler	11%	11%	56%	22%
Version Control	11%	56%	11%	22%

I learned the required skills for maintaining programs?				
	Strongly Agree	Agree	Disagree	Strongly Disagree
	22%	22%	56%	0%
Coding Documentation	0%	44%	56%	0%
Design Reviews	22%	33%	33%	11%
Code Reviews	22%	33%	33%	11%

I thought I was prepared in college for the workplace?				
	Strongly Agree	Agree	Disagree	Strongly Disagree
	11%	67%	11%	11%

Appendix D: Research Data – Software Development Team Member Interview Questions

The following interview questions were used to obtain research data from a software development team to identify gaps in skills required to design and build modern Enterprise web applications. The interview with selected members of a software development team was conducted face to face.

Question	Interviewee Responses	Gaps/Notes
What University or College did you or are you attending?	1. Arizona State University 2. Paradise Valley Community College 3. Arizona State University 4. Arizona State University 5. New York University and University of Phoenix	20% community college 80% major state university
What years did you attend University or College?	1. 2001-2008 2. 2008-2011 3. 1992-1998 4. 2002-2004 5. New York University - 1995 to 2000 and University of Phoenix - 2008 to 2010	20% during 1992-1998 80% during 2001-2010
What major did you receive or are you working on?	1. Bachelor's in computer science 2. Bachelor's in Computer Information Systems 3. Bachelor's in Computer Science 4. Bachelor's Computer	40% BSCS 40% BSCIS 20% BSET

	Engineering Technology 5. Bachelor's in Computer Information Systems from NYU and Bachelor's in Information Technology from UOP	
Was an internship offered to you while you were attending college? If yes, please explain what you did as an intern.	1. Yes. Department of Transportation. Doing some basic .NET development. .NET3.0, very basic web site to track project deliverables (used internally). Feels internships should be mandatory. 2. No. 3. Not aware of one thru university but thru industry contracts did an internship at Honeywell. Worked on creating ActiveX controls in VB6 use in a proprietary system used to monitor power generation. None of these technologies used were taught in school nor were the technologies ever mentioned (even in senior year of college). 4. No. 5. Yes, and took advantage of the	Internships should be mandatory. None of the technologies used in the internships were taught in school nor were the technologies ever mentioned (even in senior year of college). Implies that that the Computer Science program was not aligned with the industry and too far behind the industry.

	internship. Did internship from 1998 to 2000. Support for Bloomberg financial system. Monitoring scheduled jobs.	
What were your responsibilities for your first programming position out of college?	1. A little contract job for 3 months. Tiny web shop (mom and pop web site). But first real job was at Redflex Traffic Systems. Maintain and support a single C# application on .NET3.5. He did this for the first 8 months. Then moved to .NET development and worked on a small .NET application (was Classic ASP application). 2. Maintain .NET applications and C# based applications along with lots of PL/SQL. 3. Small department. VB6 executable for an insurance quotation system. Taking over existing code, more reliable, maintain, and some of the database maintain. Then got into web development in 2001 to take a static web site into an ASP dynamic web site. 4. Developing (both maintain and new	All interviewees maintained applications. 80% maintained web applications.

	application) web applications. Developing (both maintain and new application) Windows application. 5. Mainframe developer at AT&T for NYU. BA and QA at BofA for UoP.	
How many years have you worked professional in the industry?	1. Almost 4 years 2. Almost 2 years 3. Almost 13 years 4. Almost 7 years 5. Almost 11 years	2 to 13 years
What are your current responsibilities as a programmer?	1. Very similar to what was done first year out of college (maintaining .NET applications). 2. Maintain .NET applications and C# based applications along with lots of PL/SQL. 3. Maintain existing ASP based web applications. 4. Developing (both maintain and new application) web applications. 5. QA/Software Tester.	80% design, maintain, build web applications 20% QA
What classes from your program benefited you most and prepared you best for your first	1. Basic Object Orientated class based on Java programming language (a second-year class). Basic Electronic Processor (class on how code is executed in a	Basic OO, Data Structures. Assembly Language, Java, Java Swing, Database tables,

programming position?	processor). Senior class working in a Team (capstone class) 2 semester class where they were given a set of requirements and they generated UML uses cases, design specification, and wrote application (along with weekly presentation on status). This was a desktop application written in Java Swing. Taught some presentation skills. Took Data Structures and Algorithms (how to sort, heuristics, charting) was a good class. Took some Assembly Language that was a bit useful but not much. Took some Artificial Intelligence that was a bit useful but not much. Took some Compiler Designer that was a bit useful but not much. Took a database class (taught the basics of tables, joins) on SQL Server. Got some information on version control, SDLC basics, and source control (but some of this was learned from a TA). 2. .NET4.0 Problem	.NET4.0 Problem Analysis, C#, intro web design at UoP (HTML, CSS, JavaScript, AJAX, XML). Minimal UML, some design. AI, Compiler Design. Senior team project.

		Analysis and Systems Design class (solid fundamentals such as best coding practices, every week did a project with a design that needs to be approved then code the project). Usually projects were simple (such as a time clock and payroll system), got requirements at beginning of semester, each project built on each other.	
		3. Design documents could be either flow charts, pseudo code, or UML class diagrams (most used pseudo code and a few class diagrams) design was approved by instructor. Instructor had been in the industry and was good for the classroom Touched on UML. Design class should have forced the use of UML versus giving the students a choice. Project was based on Windows Form Application (WPF). Only touched very briefly on web forms and MVC. This is covered in the Advanced class. This	Should have been forced to use UML. Only 1 web application class with a minimal introduction to MVC. Lots of theory and not enough coding. Taught Pascal when the industry was using C/C++. Only touches on Java EE and the focus was on Java SE. UoP classes taught online and were really bad and taught bad programming principles in CSS. UoP did

		is the only web application design class for this entire program. In two weeks will be taking advanced .NET4.0 Problem Analysis and Systems Design class (covers MVC, advanced C# recursive, lists, multi-threading).	not teach ASP.NET in web design class.
		4. Lots of theory and not much coding. Took a good database class. Statistics class was helpful. Curriculum was Pascal (and not C/C++!!!) and did a few very small projects in Small Talk. A small amount of Java was also introduced. Very static web application (Java applets, simple HTML tags but was taught with wrong tag structure) and was also theory and concepts.	
		5. Most classes were Java related. Took 1 C# class and this was the most beneficial class. Not much was web based. Took a bit of Enterprise Java. Almost all focus on Java SE and a bit of Java ME. Tini-board class that was Java based that taught how	

	to software interact with some hardware. A class that introduced multiple languages (C, C++, VB.NET). 6. NYU: Basic programming classes and class on general computer information, C and Assembly class (no C++), no other classes. UOP: Web application programming class (Web 431 XML class), Web 404 was a class on HTML, CSS was an intro Web design and development, and Web 406 JavaScript, AJAX, Classic ASP was a Web design and development. UOP: Web 404 was an online class on HTML, CSS was an intro Web design and development and they were asked to create a basic page with no tools. Did not teach how to do properly (embedded all CSS in page). UOP: Web 406 was an online class on JavaScript, AJAX, Classic ASP was a Web design and development. There was no ASP.NET. UOP: Web 431 was an online class on XML	

	that was very bad because they did not provide proper concept for how XML is used, why used. UOP: Above 3 classes fine for online classes.	
What classes were missing from your program that would have prepared you better for your first programming position?	1. Not enough time spent on end-to-end projects with hands on (real world). C# and .NET. Java EE. Web application technologies (HTML, HTTP protocol, CSS, JavaScript). 2. Missing background on SDLC processes, source control. Missing a bit on code maintain and need to spend more time on this topic. Feels my web application design class would be very applicable in his program. 3. Very limited to any Microsoft based technologies. Development environments were all command line and no IDE's. No Windows programming classes. Did not have a taste for the real world when left school. Lack of guidance. Some instructors not aligned with the industry.	Not enough time on end-to-end real-world projects.

Not enough taught on .NET and Java EE. Also not enough taught on basic web technologies such as HTTP protocol, CSS, and JavaScript.

Not enough taught on SDLC process.

Professors did not have adequate real-world experience and outdated. |

	Some classes taught with grad students with many that were not qualified to teach. Lots of classes with adult students with industry experience that caused problems for younger students (adult would answer questions without input from younger students). 4. Learned a bit about the SDLC process but did not get to implement the process. More web application design and programming classes.	
	5. More design and architecture of web applications. Project lifecycle (SDLC) was missing. Professors do not have enough experience in real world environments. Missing how to write technical documentation (such as a Requirements document, Design document, Test Cases document).	
Do you feel your program was aligned with the current technologies used in our	1. No. No web application technologies. Some classes are offered but are electives (UI thought has some	80% of the interviewees said no. The interviewees programs were simply outdated

industry? If not, explain and give some examples.	basic HTML/CSS). 2. Yes, for .NET. There are tracks for Java and Java EE. There are tracks for Mobile. 3. No. Should have been Microsoft classes and Windows classes (the job market was expecting these skills). Lots of classes such as operating systems and technical writing were not aligned with the industry. Despite the exciting time (Windows 95 and the Internet) the professors brought no experience or passion into the classroom. 4. Laughed. No. First job was all .NET and Windows and only took a C# class. 5. UOP: No, way behind. See above.	and not aligned at all with the skills they needed for their first programming position.
Do you feel your program adequately prepared you to maintain, design, and program web applications? If not, explain and give some examples.	1. No. Would have to spend lots of time on my own to learn. Taught some fundamentals on code maintenance. 2. Yes, for .NET. Looking forward to advanced .NET class, PM, Advanced OO and Analysis Design class. 3. N/A web applications. Nothing on maintain	80% of the interviewees said no. The interviewees programs were simply outdated and not aligned at all with the skills they needed to maintain software.

	(version control, coding standards, etc.) 4. No. Definitely not how to maintain software. Only touched on the debugger for Java. 5. UOP: No. See above.	
Do you feel your program had enough hands-on labs to adequately prepare you for your first programming position? If not, explain and give some examples.	1. No. Very small projects and along the lines of proof of concepts. One project was on assembly language (8086). These projects were done in a group (of 5) and dominated by 1-2 people. Needs to be more 1-1 focus. 2. Yes, combination of 3 hour lecture and lab courses (30% lab time). 3. No. Had lots of System Engineering classes that were not applicable. Did several (and very simple DOS based) Pascal programs. 4. No. Again because there was not enough web based application classes. For programming classes that were taken were enough lab classes. 5. NYU: Yes. UOP: Yes, using prerecorded sessions, and adequate.	60% of interviewees said no and that more hands-on labs are needed.
How have you	1. Self-learning, Google,	Self-learning,

personally filled the education gaps to help you improve the background needed for your programming positions?	books. BSCS taught him how to learn but not what should be learned. 2. MSDN and Internet resources. Reading books on programming. 3. Filled in gaps thru books and work experience. 4. Taking training offered by company (MSDN, technical reference books, and Google searches). 5. Taken classes: Object Orientated Analysis & Design, Cloud Computing all taken in 2011. Took certifications: IIBA (International Institute of Business Analysis) taken in 2011. Took certifications: CSQA taken in 2011.	MSDN, books.
What recommendations would you make to University or College to improve the program and improve your readiness for an entry level programming position?	1. Minimize some of the elective classes (history, physiology, physics I and II, Calculus I, II, and III, Religions, etc.). More group projects that simulate a real-world project (handing out small projects in the group with a lead and then collaborating in the end to get it all working, weekly status	Recommendations: 1. Minimize some of the elective classes (history, physiology, physics I and II, Calculus I, II,

	reports, etc. to simulate corporate environment). Too much theory. More real-world projects that are aligned to web application development. Standardize on IDE, tools and teach how to use a debugger. Interview students during program and align with more vertical interests (web application, mobile). Hire professors that are not out of touch with the corporate environment (professors are there for research and not to teach programming). Bring in industry experts to the classroom to inject corporate experience. 2. Having the capability to research efficiently. A few weeks in a class for how to do research. 3. Adapt more quickly to modern and multiple programming languages (C# and Java). Leverage free version of Visual Studio. Web technologies. Teach the importance code performance.	and III, Religions, etc.). 2. More group projects. Projects should be aligned to real-world scenario and development process. 3. Standardize on tools using the same tools used in the industry. Leverage free tools offered by Microsoft for .NET.

	4. Maintaining software. More database classes. More Web application classes. 5. Teach how to comment/document/ maintain their code. Teach how to test code (including system integration testing). Teach project planning, milestones, SDLC. Teach SOA.	4. Teach the importa nce of code mainten ance and perform ance. 5. Teach more web applicat ion progra mming classes 6. Hire profess ors that have more real- world experie nce and not outdate d. Bring in industry experts into the classroo m.
What recommendatio ns would you make to corporations to	1. Formal training plans together on current technology stacks. Align technical training with current	Recommendatio ns: 1. More formal training.

help you improve your continuing education in our field?	project work. 2. Continue to push MSDN sponsored programming. Continue to offer tuition reimbursement. 3. Help donate resources and be more proactive with internship programs. 4. Offer more opportunities in technical courses. Need to get more involved in internships. 5. Incentives for new ideas.	2. Continue to push MSDN. 3. Continue to offer tuition reimbursement. 4. Be more proactive in internship programs.
Did you attend the Web Application Design 101 course?	1. Yes 2. Yes 3. Yes 4. Yes 5. Yes	Overwhelming yes.
Do you feel this class would be applicable to teach in a Computer Science program?	1. Yes 2. Yes 3. Definitely 4. Most definitely 5. Definitely.	Overwhelming yes. What was good (and missing) is that this covered the entire development process. Needed more details and labs.

Appendix E: Research Data - Web Application Design Class Curriculum Proposal

The following was the curriculum outline for a Web Application Design class. The class was given to a software development team in a corporate training room environment using Microsoft PowerPoint and an overhead projector.

- Course #1: Understand the Software Development Lifecycle (SDLC).
- Course #2: Understand how to decompose requirements during Requirements Analysis.
- Course #3: Understand the N-Layer Architecture.
- Course #4: Understand how to design the Presentation Layer. With companion lab.
- Course #5: Understand how to design the Business Services Layer. With companion lab.
- Course #6: Understand how to design the Data Access Layer. With companion lab.
- Course #7: Understand industry Best Practices.
- Course #8: Putting It All Together. With companion lab.

Appendix F: Research Data - Implementation Plan

The following implementation plan was used to execute the selected solutions outlined in the Solution Strategy from Chapter 4.

Week	Task	Notes
1	Setup and conduct the anonymous core technical skills Zoomerang Survey. Complete Web Application Design training course #1 and course #2 with the software development team.	Give the survey participants one week to respond to the survey.
2	Research the top 5 major university Computer Science program and Information Technology program. Complete Web Application Design training course #3 and course #4 with the software development team.	Assemble findings from the university Computer Science program and Information Technology program programs class curriculum and labs.
3	Setup and conduct the anonymous maintenance skills Zoomerang Survey. Complete Web Application Design training course #5 and course #6 with the software development team.	Assemble findings from the core technical skills survey. Give the survey participants one week to respond to the survey.
4	Contact the face-to-face interviewees to schedule an interview over the next two weeks. Complete Web Application Design training course #7 and course #8 with the software development team.	Assemble findings from the maintenance skills survey.
5 - 6	Conduct face-to-face interviews.	
7 - 8	Assemble findings from the face-to-face interviews. Assemble findings from training course	

9 - 12	Write Action Research Project	

www.ingramcontent.com/pod-product-compliance
Lightning Source LLC
Chambersburg PA
CBHW030914180526
45163CB00004B/1829